Time to play I Spy Animals

Edwin Kim

Ilustrated by
Mayara Nogueira

COPYRIGHT © ASCEND DIGITAL
ALL RIGHTS RESERVED

Can you spot the animal that begins with the letter B or F? Find the animal that matches each letter, then turn the page and see if you've chosen correctly!

Enjoy this fun spy activity with, "Time To Play I Spy Animals.

Animals

RABBIT

DEER

SQUIRREL

MOUSE

FROG

BADGER

SNAKE

MOLE

EAGLE

 WOLF
 MOOSE
 TURTLE
 SKUNK
 RACCOON
 OWL
 HEDGEHOG
 FOX
 BOAR

 BEAR

B is for...

BADGER

B is for...

BEAR

B is for...

BOAR

D is for...

DEER

E is for...

EAGLE

F is for...

FOX

H is for...

HEDGEHOG

M is for...

MOLE

M is for...

MOOSE

M is for...

MOUSE

O is for...

OWL

R is for...
RABBIT

R is for...

RACCOON

S is for...

SNAKE

S is for...

SKUNK

T is for...

TURTLE

W is for...

WOLF

Author

Edwin Kim
edwinkim.co

Edwin Kim is a creative entrepreneur who loves to create inspirational books that can bring valuable lessons to the next generation. He happily creates stories and loves to bring his ideas to life.

Ilustrator

Mayara Nogueira
artstation.com/mayaranogueira

Mayara is passionate about the world of illustrated books. She loves drawing animal, historical and fantasy themes.

www.ingramcontent.com/pod-product-compliance
Lightning Source LLC
Chambersburg PA
CBHW040109120526
44589CB00041B/2991